GREAT CAKE OFF

Steve Barlow and Steve Skidmore

Illustrated by Alex Lopez

Franklin Watts
First published in Great Britain in 2017 by The Watts Publishing Group

Credits
Executive Editor: Adrian Cole
Design Manager: Peter Scoulding
Cover Designer: Cathryn Gilbert
Illustrations: Alex Lopez

HB ISBN 978 1 4451 5379 7
PB ISBN 978 1 4451 5381 0
Library ebook ISBN 978 1 4451 5380 3

Printed in China.

MIX
Paper from
responsible sources
FSC
www.fsc.org FSC® C104740

Franklin Watts
An imprint of
Hachette Children's Group
Part of The Watts Publishing Group
Carmelite House
50 Victoria Embankment
London EC4Y 0DZ

An Hachette UK Company
www.hachette.co.uk

www.franklinwatts.co.uk

Lin

Danny

Sam

"You have two days," said Mr Broad.

"The best cake baker will win a prize.

Get ready and bake!"

"My angel cake will win," said Britney.

"No chance," said Clogger. "My prize

muffins will win."

"You are a prize muffin!" laughed Lin.

"Ha, ha," said Clogger. "You three
will lose."

"We'll see about that," said Lin.

"Come on you two!"

Finally, the other cakes were baked.

"Do you like my fairy cakes?" said Lin.

Sam and Danny tried one.

"Yuk! They've got dog hairs in!" said Sam.

"They're hairy, fairy cakes," laughed Danny.

"Do you like my sponge fingers?"
said Sam

Danny and Lin tasted them.

"Is it thumbs up? Or is it thumbs down?"
asked Sam.

"No," replied Lin. "It's thumbs in!"

She held up Sam's thumb.

"Ooops," said Sam. "I wondered where
they were."

...ary

...51

...21/02/2020 13:46

XXXXX3126

Bor...

Item Ti...		Due Date
...x and the snow		13/03/2020
* Pop...		
dog ...Beauty = La Bella		13/03/2020
* Sle...		
Du/dinner		13/03/2020
* ...ntures of the Furry		13/03/2020
...edom Fighters		
Happy Mouseday		13/03/2020
* broom to go zoom		13/03/2020
* Pigsticks and Harold and the incredible journey		13/03/2020
* flamingo who forgot		13/03/2020
* Great cake off		13/03/2020
* Flight of the winged serpent : a Cretaceous adventure		13/03/2020
* Scorpion strike		13/03/2020
* Rainbow Dash's big race!		13/03/2020

* indicates items borrowed today

www.bromley.gov.uk

"It looks better than ours," said Britney.

"Don't worry," replied Clogger. "I'll make sure they don't win…"